The Telephone

Almost from the time you first open your eyes in this modern
world, you see people using the telephone, and before many years
pass you are using it yourself. But how does it work? Haven't
you often stopped to wonder at the miracle that lets you talk to
someone miles away?

To explain the telephone, this book uses many familiar ideas
and suggests simple experiments which you yourself can carry
out with a little help from parent or teacher.

From the general idea of what a sound is, Henry Brinton goes
on to explain the speaking tube. Then there is a description of
an easily made mechanical telephone, followed by the electro-
magnet and Edison's wonderful discovery of a practical telephone.

Finding Out

About SCIENCE

Edited by

KURT ROWLAND

THE TELEPHONE

by HENRY BRINTON

Illustrated by BERNARD LODGE

Golden Press ⚡ New York

THIS EDITION PUBLISHED 1966 BY GOLDEN PRESS, INC., NEW YORK.

Library of Congress Catalog
Card Number 62-9349

Contents

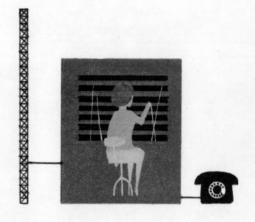

From the time when men wore skins and lived in caves they have wanted to send messages to one another. Perhaps they did it by sending smoke signals, as the American Indians were still doing a few hundred years ago.

6

Primitive people in Africa still send messages to each other over very long distances by beating drums, whose noise can be heard a long way off. Fires, too, have been used for sending very simple messages. For instance, when the attack by the

ships of the great Spanish Armada was expected, huge bonfires were prepared all over England, each of which was just in sight of the next one. When the Armada was sighted, the first fire was lit, then the second and so on—and soon they were blazing all over England. There is a poem by Lord Macaulay which tells how within a few hours of the time when the ships were first seen, everyone in England knew that the Armada was on the way and that it was time to get their arms and be ready to fight.

This sort of signaling works very well for the simplest kind of message. For instance, when the fire alarm sounds everyone who hears it knows that there is a fire; but it cannot tell you much about the fire, or how big it is. You cannot ask questions about the fire and get answers.

About a century and a half ago, a better way of passing on messages was invented. This was called the *semaphore*. There were tall towers, each just in sight of the next, and there were arms on top of each tower, which could be moved from inside. By putting the arms into different positions, representing different letters, any message one liked could be spelled out and sent as far as the chains of towers reached.

For short distances semaphore is still sometimes used for signaling by two men holding flags in their hands, especially between two ships within sight of one another.

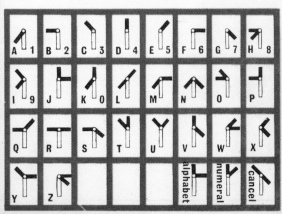

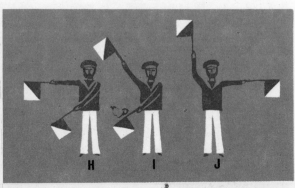

A little later, after men were beginning to understand electricity, they found out how to send messages along wires by using electric currents. Quite soon, wires stretched not only over Europe and America, but all over the world, going under the sea, right across the largest oceans. People on the other side of the world could get a message a few minutes after it was sent off.

This method, which is called the *electric telegraph*, had been talked about for a hundred years before anyone managed to make one which worked usefully. It might have been done sooner, but men seem to delay making new inventions until they become necessary. It was about a century ago that the need for a really quick way of sending and receiving messages, whatever the weather was like, became urgent. Because of all the new machines, and especially of the railways, which were coming into use more rapidly every year, the speed of life was becoming so great that we just *had* to have some way of signaling which was quick and safe. The electric telegraph was invented because we needed it so badly.

You probably know how an electric flashlight works. There is a battery of cells and a bulb, with a switch which you push when you want the flashlight to shine. The switch is only a sort of faucet which allows the current to flow from the battery through the bulb when it is pressed—just as water flows into a basin when the faucet is turned on.

Electricity can work only when it is allowed to flow from one end of the cell or battery of cells, through wires, and return to the other end. This is called a *circuit*. When a break is made in the circuit, the electric current will stop flowing.

An electric light switch does just that. If you wish to switch your light off, you move a little lever on the switch or press a button. This breaks the circuit and the light goes out.

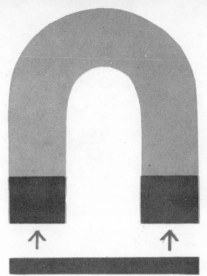

The secret of the telegraph is the *electro-magnet*. You will know about an ordinary magnet, which is made of magnetized steel and picks up bits of iron such as needles. An electro-magnet is just a magnet which works by electricity, and you can make one for yourself.

All you need is a small bar of soft iron, a lot of the right kind of thin insulated wire from an electrician, and some electric cells with convenient terminals. If you wind the right amount of wire—the electrician will tell you how much, depending on what cells you are using—round and round the iron bar, and join each end of the wire to one terminal of the cells, you will find that you have a magnet which will pick up needles. You will also find that, the moment you undo one of the ends of the wire from the cells, the needles will fall off. The iron will be a magnet only as long as electricity is flowing around it from the cells.

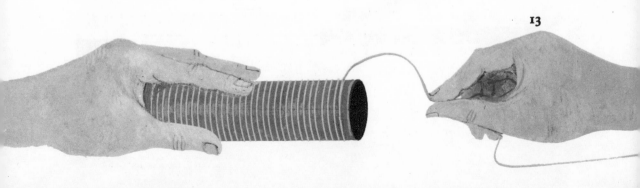

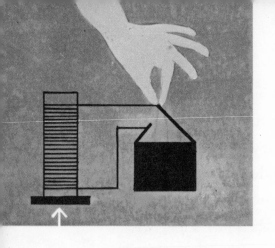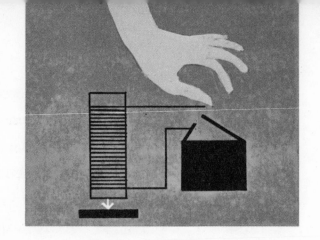

But joining and undoing wires is quite awkward if you have to do it often. An instrument like the one shown at the foot of this page is used instead. If you follow the wire you will see that when the lever, which is called a key, is pressed down, the circuit will be closed and the electro-magnet will work. When the lever is allowed to go up, the circuit will be broken. It works just like a light switch.

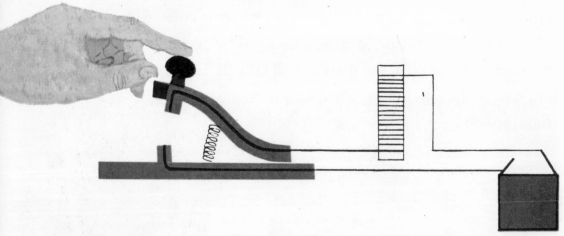

In the electric telegraph, the key is at the sending station and an electro-magnet is used to move a pointer at the receiving end of the line. This in turn can be made to move a pen, as in the picture, which will make a mark on a moving strip of paper.

If the lever is pressed down for a very short time and then allowed to come up again, the pen will make a dot on the strip of paper. If the lever is held down for a little longer, the pen will make a dash on the paper.

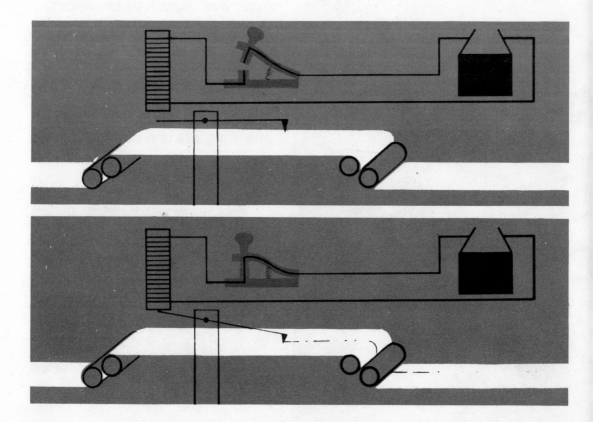

A	● ▬	M	▬ ▬	Y	▬ ● ▬ ▬
B	▬ ● ● ●	N	▬ ●	Z	▬ ▬ ● ●
C	▬ ● ▬ ●	O	▬ ▬ ▬	1	● ▬ ▬ ▬ ▬
D	▬ ● ●	P	● ▬ ▬ ●	2	● ● ▬ ▬ ▬
E	●	Q	▬ ▬ ● ▬	3	● ● ● ▬ ▬
F	● ● ▬ ●	R	● ▬ ●	4	● ● ● ● ▬
G	▬ ▬ ●	S	● ● ●	5	● ● ● ● ●
H	● ● ● ●	T	▬	6	▬ ● ● ● ●
I	● ●	U	● ● ▬	7	▬ ▬ ● ● ●
J	● ▬ ▬ ▬	V	● ● ● ▬	8	▬ ▬ ▬ ● ●
K	▬ ● ▬	W	● ▬ ▬	9	▬ ▬ ▬ ▬ ●
L	● ▬ ● ●	X	▬ ● ● ▬	0	▬ ▬ ▬ ▬ ▬

The idea of using groups of dots and dashes to represent letters of the alphabet is due to a famous American, Samuel F. B. Morse, and the system is called the Morse code after him. On May 24th, 1844, he sent the historic message: "What hath God wrought!" from Washington to Baltimore by telegraph.

Although electric telegraphs had been in use on English railways since 1837, Morse's invention made sending messages

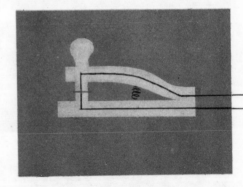

very much easier and simpler, and his code is used for many purposes. You can use it yourself for sending messages by flashlight.

The invention of the electric telegraph was a great step forward in the art of communication. Messages could be sent quickly over great distances. It made it possible for trains to travel safely at great speeds as it took only a few moments to send warnings of danger from one signal box to another.

On New Year's Day, 1845, soon after it had been installed on the Great Western Railway, a murder was committed at Slough,

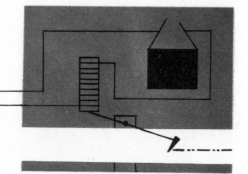

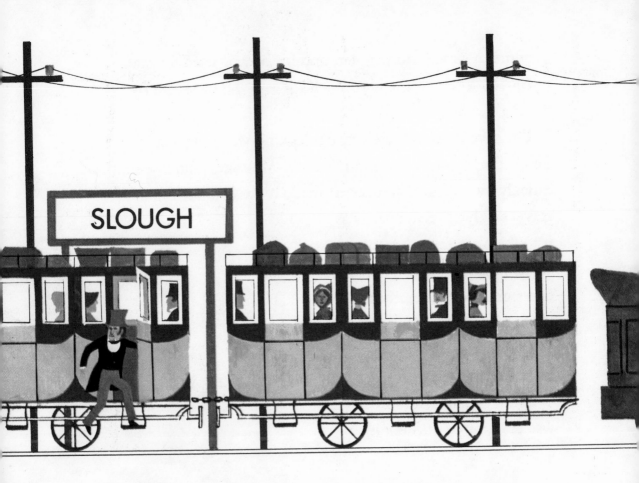

20 miles from London. A man suspected of the crime was
seen getting into a train for London. A message was sent by
the new electric telegraph and a Railway Police detective met
the train at Paddington Station, in London, recognized the
man from the telegraphed description, and followed him. Later
on he was arrested and convicted of the murder.

Though the telegraph was already doing wonderful work every day in protecting the lives of railway passengers, this capture of a criminal made people sit up and take notice of the new invention. Without the telegraph the murderer might easily have got away. Very soon a network of telegraphs covered many countries.

This was all very wonderful; but having to write out messages to send them by telegraph was still a clumsy way of "talking" to someone a long way off. From the time that the electric telegraph was invented, men dreamed of being able to *talk* to one another at great distances, and it was only a very short time before the first experiments with telephones were made.

But, before we go any further, let us think about how we hear at all—about what a sound is.

Sounds, as we hear them normally, are made by movements of the air; if there were no air, we should hear no sounds. We can prove this by putting a bell under a glass bowl and ringing it. The bell can still be heard; but, if you use an air pump, and take the air out from under the bowl, the sound of the bell gets less as the air is sucked out. When nearly all the air has gone, you will not be able to hear the bell at all, because there is nothing to carry the sound. Your father or school teacher

may be able to perform this experiment for you.

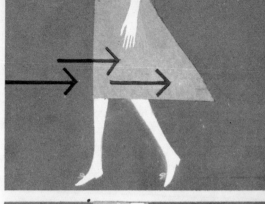

Air is something quite real, even though we cannot see it. We can feel it, by putting our heads out of a moving car or train; and we can see its effect, when it blows a woman's skirt in the wind in just the same way as it would be caught if she walked through very long grass or low bushes.

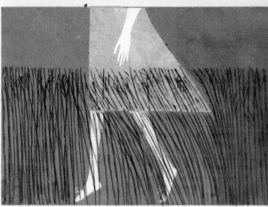

When air is suddenly squashed up—*compressed*, we call it— a sound is made. You can make a paper clapper and see for yourself that this is true. The picture shows you how to do it.

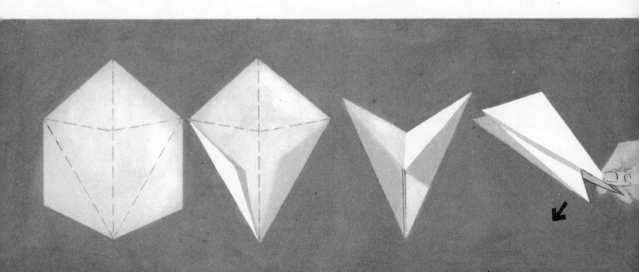

Why is this? It is because waves are made in the air, rather as waves are made in water when we drop a stone into a pool. Let us think for a moment about a sheet of metal, and see what happens when we strike it. The force of the blow makes the metal tremble to and fro. This is called *vibrating*. The string of a harp or guitar also vibrates when we pluck it.

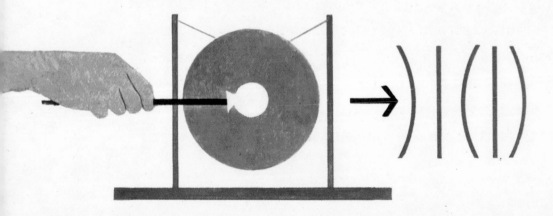

As the sheet of metal vibrates, it first pushes the air
forward and then sucks it back again, all very quickly, so that
little ripples, or waves, are made which travel away from the
metal in all directions. You can actually see the sort of thing
which is happening if you take a long loose coil spring with
large coils and hang it up. If you hit one end with the flat of
your hand, you will see a ripple pass right along the spring.

These waves in the air are so tiny that you cannot feel them.
Just the same, you can tell that they are there because they will
make another sheet of metal vibrate when they hit it—not as
hard, of course, but still just enough to hear the second sheet
vibrate although you have not touched it. Try hanging two
sheets of metal of the same size and shape facing one another.
Hit the first and make it ring, then put your hand on it to
stop the vibrations. If you listen carefully, you will hear the
second sheet of metal vibrating faintly.

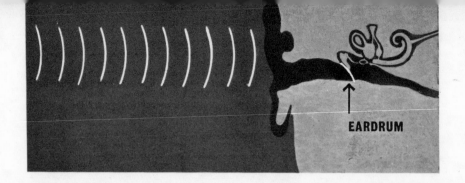

EARDRUM

This is how we hear a noise. The first sheet is behaving like the vocal cords in our throats, which we move when we speak and set vibrating. They make tiny waves in the air which hit the drums of our ears and set them vibrating, just as the second sheet was set vibrating. When that happens we hear a noise.

The earliest telephones were simple speaking tubes. You can see in the picture below how they worked. The tube stopped the sound waves from spreading in all directions, so they reached much farther in the one direction in which they were allowed to travel.

Telephones like this did not carry over great distances, but they were good enough for speaking from one story of a house to another.

Try this out for yourself with a long tube or even a flexible tube like one on a vacuum cleaner, if it is not too dirty.

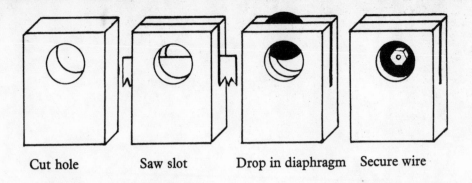

Cut hole   Saw slot   Drop in diaphragm   Secure wire

There is a second kind of telephone which you could make for yourself. Cut the bottoms out of two tin cans with a can-opener, and fasten each of them into a wooden frame, as shown in the picture. Then fasten a long piece of thin wire to the middle of each piece of tin can with a small nut and bolt which you can get at a hardware shop—and there you have a telephone, so long as the wire is stretched out tight. One person talks into one piece of tin can—this is called a *diaphragm*—and the other person puts his ear to the other. In this way you can hear each other several hundred yards away if the wire is that long.

When you speak into the first diaphragm, you make it vibrate. The wire carries the vibration by little tugs and makes the far diaphragm vibrate in exactly the same way. That makes new waves of the same kind in the air, and so the other person hears what you say.

Though this is a telephone, it is not much use except
as a toy, because it will work for only a short way. A real
telephone uses electricity in a simple way to transfer the
vibrations along the wire instead of letting the wire do it by
little tugs.

Many people helped to invent the telephone, but the greatest
discovery was made by a Scotsman called Alexander Graham
Bell, who had gone to live in the United States. He wanted to
help deaf and dumb children, and so he began to study how
sounds are made and carried. Strangely enough, he stumbled
on the secret of the electric telephone by accident.

His telephone was greatly improved by another American
inventor, Thomas A. Edison; and the Edison-Bell telephone
that we use today is still the same *sort* of telephone.

Suppose you take your home-made electro-magnet and hold

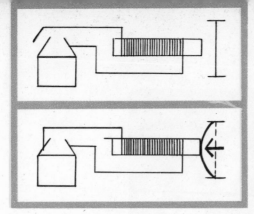

In the top picture, one wire is not connected to the battery so there is no current and the diaphragm is flat. In the bottom picture, the current makes the iron bar a magnet, and the diaphragm is bent toward it

it over a needle and keep on joining up the wire to the battery and taking it off again, the needle will jump up and down. Suppose now that, instead of a needle, you hold the magnet near to a diaphragm—your piece of tin can, for instance. Every time you join up the wire, it will draw the diaphragm very slightly toward the magnet, and every time you loosen the wire, it will spring back again. If you could do it fast enough—more than 30 times a second—the diaphragm would vibrate in time with the electric current coming and going, and make *sound waves* which you could hear. In this way sounds can be made by electricity. If the current comes and goes in the right way, it will make any sound you like—even a human voice.

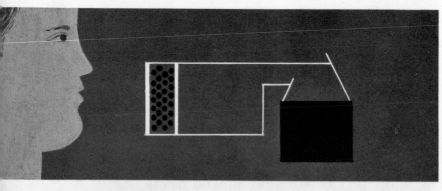

Carbon grains
loose: little flow
of current

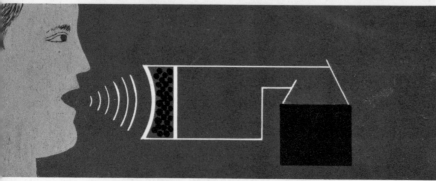

Carbon grains
compressed by
sound wave: flow
of current increases

What Edison discovered was that an electric current will
pass through grains of carbon more easily when they are
pressed up together than when they are loose. *Carbon*, as
you probably know, is only charcoal, or the lead of a lead
pencil. If you put a diaphragm up against a packed lump
of carbon grains with an electric current going through them,
and then talk into the diaphragm, you can see what will happen.
As the diaphragm vibrates with the sound of the voice, it will

squash the carbon up and let it loose again in time with the
vibrations of your voice on the diaphragm. When the carbon
grains are compressed, a lot of electricity will flow through them;
when they are loosened, less electricity will get through. If the
current is then taken along wires for even a very long way, and

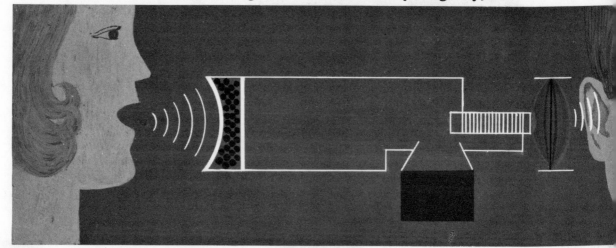

then passed around the wires of an electro-magnet in front of
another diaphragm, it will make that one vibrate in exactly
the same way. That is to say it will make a sound exactly like
your voice talking into the other end a long, long way away.
That was the way that the Edison-Bell telephone worked when
it was first invented. And that is more or less how it
works today when you speak to someone even in another
continent.

Bell's telephone

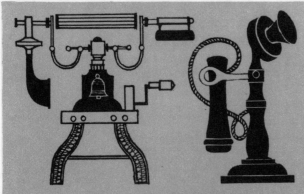

Different kinds of
telephones of the
last century

An early public
telephone

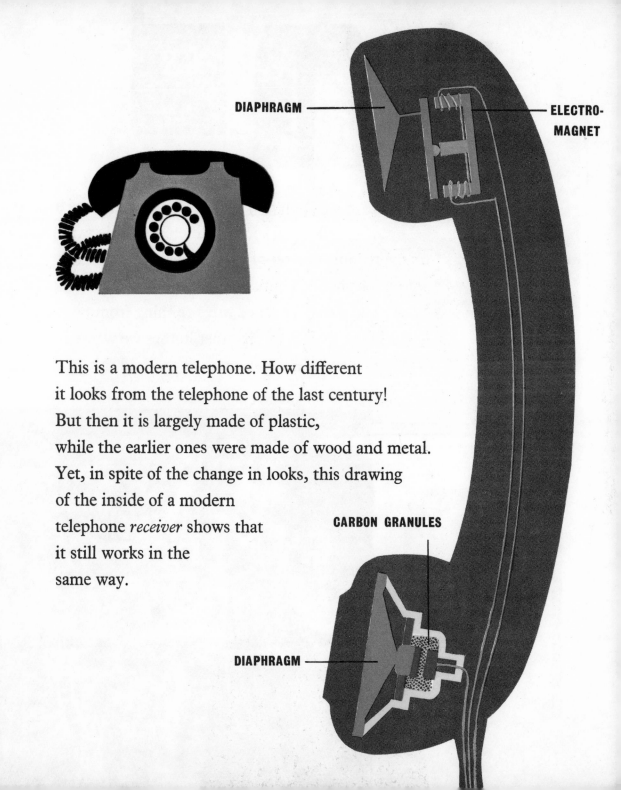

DIAPHRAGM

ELECTRO-MAGNET

This is a modern telephone. How different
it looks from the telephone of the last century!
But then it is largely made of plastic,
while the earlier ones were made of wood and metal.
Yet, in spite of the change in looks, this drawing
of the inside of a modern
telephone *receiver* shows that
it still works in the
same way.

CARBON GRANULES

DIAPHRAGM

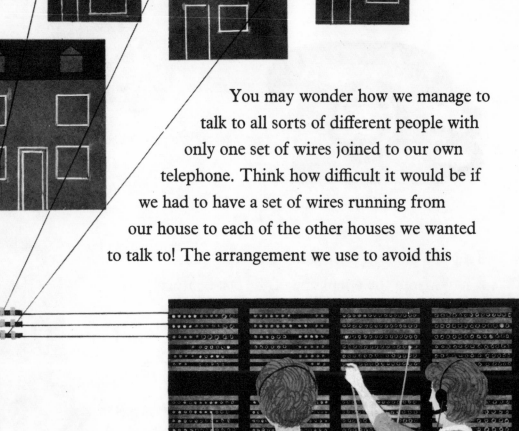

You may wonder how we manage to
talk to all sorts of different people with
only one set of wires joined to our own
telephone. Think how difficult it would be if
we had to have a set of wires running from
our house to each of the other houses we wanted
to talk to! The arrangement we use to avoid this

is quite simple. Each telephone has its own set of wires running
to what is called a *telephone exchange* or central office. At the
exchange a light is lit up when you pick up your receiver,
and this tells the operator that you want to speak to her.

Your wire ends on the operator's board in a "jack" or

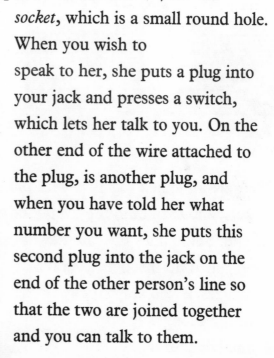

socket, which is a small round hole.
When you wish to
speak to her, she puts a plug into
your jack and presses a switch,
which lets her talk to you. On the
other end of the wire attached to
the plug, is another plug, and
when you have told her what
number you want, she puts this
second plug into the jack on the
end of the other person's line so
that the two are joined together
and you can talk to them.

33

If the person you want to talk to lives a long way off, he will be connected to a different exchange; but the operator at your end will have a line to this other exchange. The drawing shows that, if the two exchanges are a long distance apart, yet a third exchange may have to be asked to take part in the link-up.

They are all joined together with plugs and sockets, and then onto the telephone at the far end. Sometimes the call may have to be joined up through several exchanges, if you are ringing someone a long way off in another country.

Nowadays, the connection is usually made by dialing the number you want, without an operator having any part in joining the lines together.

An automatic exchange

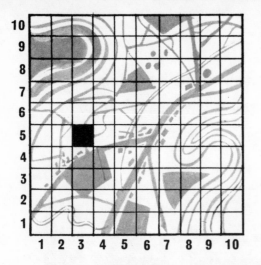

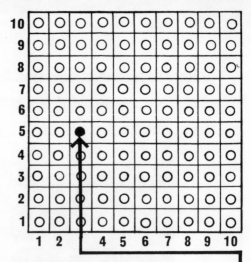

It seems magical, but actually a dialing system is quite simple. It is similar to finding a spot on a large map which is divided up into squares like the one in this picture. If you are told that the place you are looking for is in square 35 you will move along 3 squares and up 5. This will get you to the right square.

At the exchange we can imagine a board with sockets in it, arranged in rows, as shown in the picture. When you turned the dial on your telephone the plug on the end of your line would go across as many rows as the first number you had dialed. If, for instance, you dialed 3, the plug would go across 3 rows. The second number you dialed would move it up the chosen row, so that if your second number were 5, the plug would move up 5 holes. This would connect it with the socket belonging to the line of the person you were calling. Actually it is not

quite as simple as that; but it gives an idea of the *way* it works.
As I have described it, you could only pick one of a hundred
lines, and no one else could use the board at the same time.
In a real dial system, where you turn your dial several times,
the number of lines you can pick is multiplied by 10 every
time you turn it. So it becomes 1,000 when you twist your
dial for the third number, 10,000 for the fourth, etc. And
other people can use the same board at the same time. This
kind of exchange is called an automatic exchange.

Not many years after the invention of the electric telegraph,
wires, called cables, were laid under the sea, even under the
wide oceans between continents. Laying these cables was very
difficult in the early days in very deep water—sometimes miles
deep. Crossing the Atlantic between England and America was
the first great test, and it was successful only because there
was a huge ship called the Great Eastern, much the largest
ship in the world, which could be used.

Cable system between America and Europe

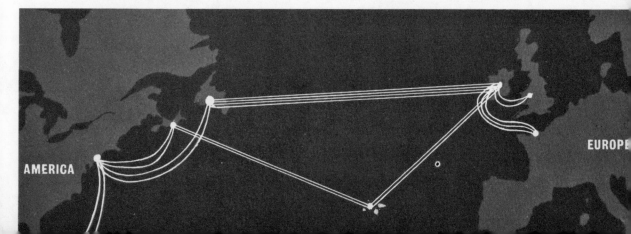

AMERICA

EUROPE

Nowadays we use ships specially built for laying cables, and the cables themselves are specially protected with many separate coverings. You can see that the cable has to be laid over all kinds of unevenness—even over mountains—under the sea. An accurate map must be made of where the cable is, so that it can easily be found again when repairs are needed.

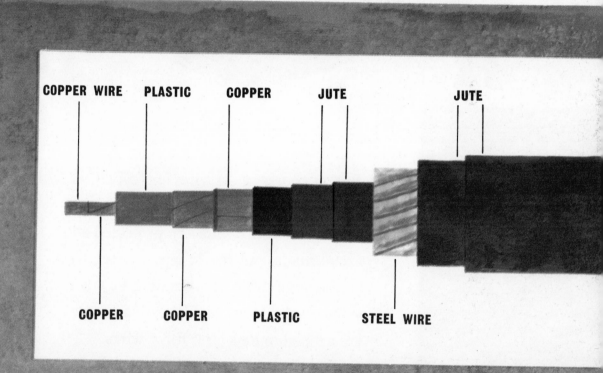

COPPER WIRE   PLASTIC   COPPER   JUTE   JUTE

COPPER   COPPER   PLASTIC   STEEL WIRE

But, of course, most wires and cables are laid overland. When they are buried underground they must be protected and are normally put inside pipes. Often there are many of these lines running together side by side. Many highly skilled people are needed to look after these wires. Can you imagine what a difficult job it must be to join all the wires together without getting mixed up?

Many wires are carried on poles.
When new wires have to be added
or old ones repaired, a man has to
climb to the top of a pole. There are
brackets fixed to the side of the pole
which make it quite easy for him to
get to the top. But you may have
noticed that the brackets start only
part of the way up and he
has to reach the lowest with a ladder. This is to stop children
from trying to climb the pole.

There are many marvels of science used for telephones these days. One of them is hard to believe. A whole lot of people can talk to one another over the same line, without any of them hearing the others except for the one they want. A man in Edinburgh, for example, may be talking to a man in New York over the same line that a woman in London is using to talk to another in Montreal, as well as a dozen others.

You can get a general idea of how this is done by an experiment you can make for yourself if you borrow some *tuning forks* from your school music teacher. You will need two pairs of tuning forks, two each of two different notes, which we will call A and C. If you strike one of the A notes near the other A and a C, you will find that the other A will give out a

faint note; but not the C tuning fork. It is almost as though the
C tuning fork had not heard. The C fork will make the second
C fork vibrate and make a sound; but not the A.

Now try to think of sending messages through a speaking
tube with tuning forks. You might be sending a series of notes
through the tube with an A fork, which could be picked up at
the other end by someone with another A fork. At the same time
two other people could be signaling through the same tube
using C forks. By using electric currents of different "notes"
in a similar way many people can use the same wire for
speaking to each other.

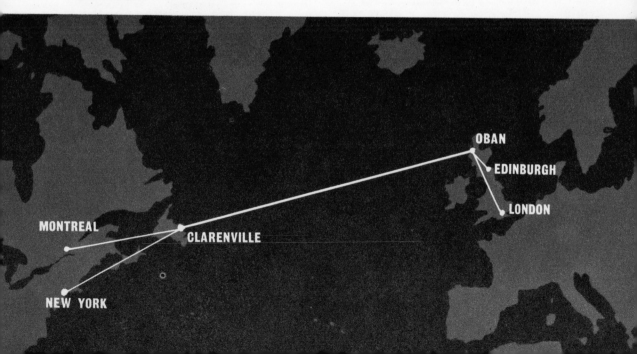

A radio station used for sending messages

It was not long after telephones came into general use that Marconi made the first radio transmitters for sending Morse. Soon, it was discovered how to send speech too without wires, and the first transatlantic telephones used a radio link. Though cables are better, and we now have telephone cables across the Atlantic, we use radio to talk to one another in ships and planes. A service has even been started by which, in some places, you can have a radio telephone in your car and talk to other people in other cars, or in their homes and offices.

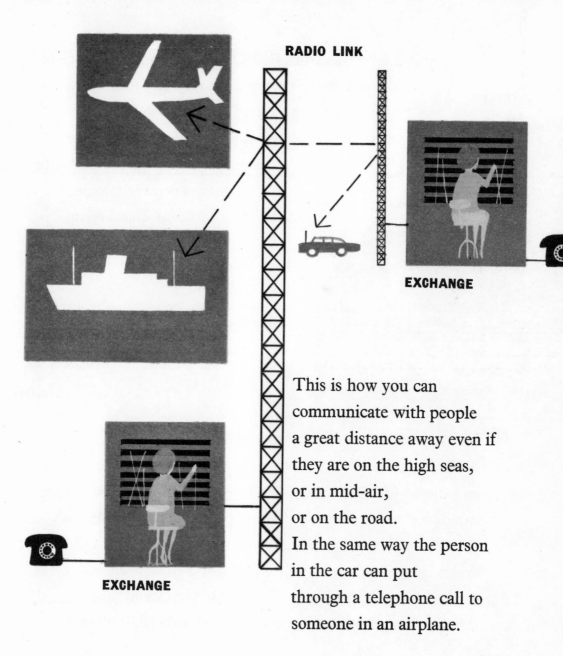

RADIO LINK

EXCHANGE

EXCHANGE

This is how you can
communicate with people
a great distance away even if
they are on the high seas,
or in mid-air,
or on the road.
In the same way the person
in the car can put
through a telephone call to
someone in an airplane.

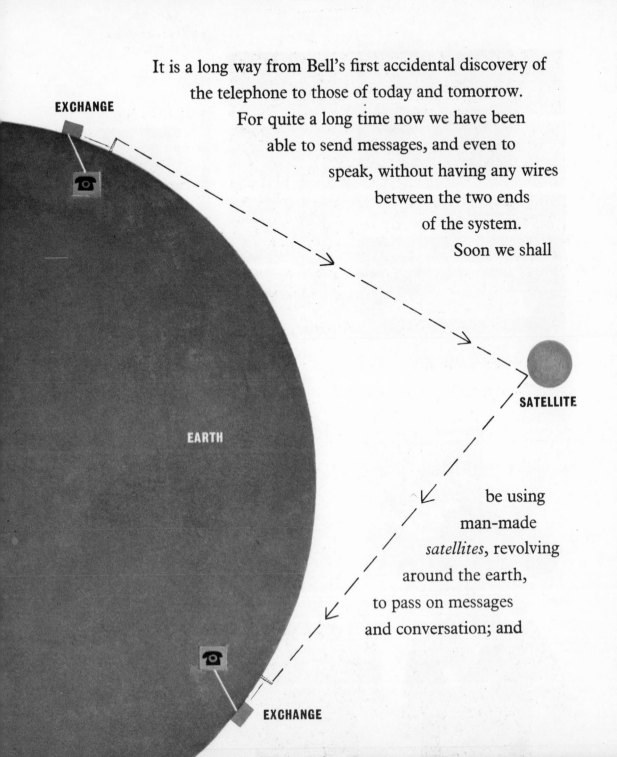

It is a long way from Bell's first accidental discovery of
the telephone to those of today and tomorrow.
For quite a long time now we have been
able to send messages, and even to
speak, without having any wires
between the two ends
of the system.
Soon we shall

EXCHANGE

SATELLITE

EARTH

be using
man-made
satellites, revolving
around the earth,
to pass on messages
and conversation; and

EXCHANGE

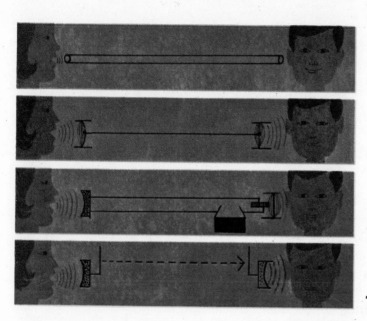

The four major stages of the telephone

The speaking tube

The mechanical telephone

The electric telephone

The radio link

even pictures, cheaply, quickly and easily; but the telephone mouthpiece and receiver are still almost exactly the same as Edison and Bell made them so long ago. They might be very surprised if they could come back and see the wonderful uses to which their simple invention has been put.

Some of the new words which you read in this book.

Carbon. Lamp-black and the lead of pencils are forms of carbon, which is very common in nature.

Circuit (SIR kit). The path around which an electric current flows.

Compress (kom PRESS). Press together.

Diaphragm (DY a fram). A thin plate, usually of metal.

Electro-magnet. A magnet which is made by an electric current passing around and around a piece of iron.

Electric telegraph. A way of sending messages by an electric current, carried along wires.

Receiver. In a telephone the receiver is the part which we put to our ear to listen to the other person talking.

Satellite (SAT el lite). A body which circles around the Earth or some other planet.

Semaphore (SEM a for). A way of signaling with arms – whether they are our own or arms on top of towers.

Socket. A round hole into which a peg can be fitted.

Sound waves. Movements of the air which make sounds when they reach our ears.

Telephone Exchange. A place where telephone lines from houses and offices are taken so that they can be connected with each other.

Tuning fork. A metal fork which makes the sound of a particular note when it is struck.

Vibrate (VY brate). Shake rapidly to and fro.